A Forest Community

Written by Elizabeth Massie

STECK-VAUGHN
ELEMENTARY · SECONDARY · ADULT · LIBRARY

A Harcourt Classroom Education Company

Contents

Chapter	Page
1 What Is a Temperate Forest Community?	3
2 Oh, Deer!	7
3 Whooo Lives in That Tree?	12
4 Busy Builders	17
5 Burrows and Pouches	22
6 T-T-Termites!	26
7 The Forest Community and People	30
Glossary	31
Index	32

Chapter 1

What Is a Temperate Forest Community?

A family lives in a house on the edge of a small but busy town. The family likes being part of a **community**. There is a grocer who sells food. There are police officers and firefighters that keep citizens safe. There are doctors, dentists, teachers, and librarians, all who help make the neighborhood a pleasant place to live.

Beyond the family's backyard lies another kind of community that is also full of life and activity. This neighborhood is a **temperate** forest.

The plants and animals in this forest are helpful to one another. Oak trees provide homes for robins. The birds eat seeds and drop some on the ground. Then earthworms loosen the soil and make it easier for new plants to grow.

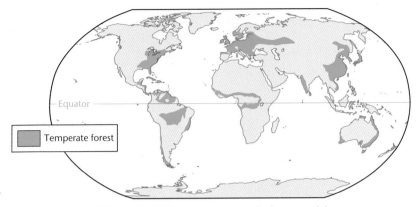

Equator

Temperate forest

Temperate forests around the world

Temperate forests are found in different places around the world, including some parts of North America and South America, Europe, Asia, Africa, and Australia. The word *temperate* means mild. In a temperate forest, it may get cold—as low as 20°F (-7°C). It may get hot—as high as 85°F (+30°C). But these temperatures are not as severe as in other places such as deserts and Arctic regions.

Because of the mild temperatures, temperate forests have long growing seasons, which last five to six months during spring and summer. The growing season is the time when plants put out new leaves and begin to grow. Animals such as woodchucks and beavers eat these plants. The animals put on extra layers of fat from eating so much during the growing season.

A fox drinks from a stream.

A caribou has huge antlers.

The growing season usually ends once the fall arrives. Then most plants of the temperate forest stop growing until the next spring. Trees such as maples, oaks, and beech shed their leaves in the fall. Insects such as millipedes and mites find shelter beneath the fallen leaves. The leaves will decay and help form new, rich soil in which plants will grow when it is warm again.

Some of the animals of this forest stay active during the cold months, eating foods such as berries and nuts that they stored during the growing season. Other animals such as bears **hibernate**, or are not active, during winter. They must survive on the fat in their bodies.

5

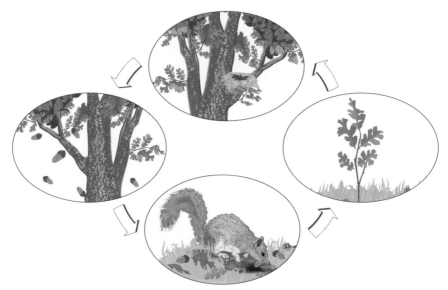

Plants and animals help each other.

The plants help the animals, and the animals help the plants. All living things in the temperate forest community work together in their own unique ways. An acorn that a gray squirrel buries may be forgotten and left in the ground, only to grow into a brand new oak tree. Later, the tree grows acorns, which turn brown and fall to the ground. Then a gray squirrel buries an acorn again!

The interesting community that lives in a temperate forest is worth a closer look!

Chapter 2

Oh, Deer!

Blooming at the edge of the forest is a patch of red clover. A **herd** of white-tailed deer look out to make sure there is no danger, and then they graze on the clover.

A white-tailed deer is often seen in temperate forests. In the summer, the deer has a short, thick, reddish-brown coat made of stiff hairs. But in winter, the deer grows a thick coat with longer hairs that are hollow like tiny straws. These hairs trap the air warmed by the deer's body and help keep the animal comfortable even on the coldest nights.

A full-grown male deer is called a buck. A full-grown female deer is called a doe. A buck is normally larger than a doe.

A doe will have one or two babies in late spring. The babies are called fawns. They weigh about six pounds (three kilograms) and are covered with white spots. These spots help protect them from enemies. When fawns lie quietly in the grass, they look like patches of ground with sunlight on them.

Fawns grow quickly. By the time they are four months old, they will be as big as their mothers. At one year old, they are full grown.

Deer eat many different things in the temperate forest. In the spring, summer, and fall they enjoy grasses, twigs, fruits, acorns, buds, and mushrooms.

Fawns have white spots to help protect them.

Deer eat much like cows. They chew their cud. After feeding, a deer will look for a safe resting spot and lie down. Then it will force the food, now called cud, from its stomach back into its mouth. Each piece of cud will get about 40 chews, and then the deer will swallow it again.

In winter, a deer will use its hooves to uncover moss and leaves to find food. When winter snow is too deep, the deer will eat bark or twigs from trees.

A buck eats bark from a tree.

White-tailed deer live in a herd.

Deer do not travel far from their **territory**, the area where they live, unless the area begins to run out of food. One deer's territory is about the size of 400 football fields. Up to thirty or more deer can share a territory this size when there is plenty of food for all of them.

Unlike many smaller animals, white-tailed deer do not build nests or dens. Instead, they will rest in any place that seems safe and is comfortable. Usually, this will be an area that is dry and surrounded by trees.

In winter, deer will often look for a place with low-hanging pine or spruce branches to rest beneath. Resting under these tree branches helps the deer blend in with the surroundings so they are safe from their enemies.

Only a male white-tailed deer grows antlers, which are called a rack. The buck will grow a new rack every year. Antlers are used to fight other male deer to keep them away.

Antlers begin to grow in the spring. By late summer, they are full grown. In the winter, the antlers fall off. They break off near the buck's head and may leave sore spots for a while. Antlers that have fallen off provide a tasty treat for other animals in the forest. Chipmunks and mice will nibble on them. Insects will also eat them.

On a summer evening, a young buck stops by a maple tree and cleans its antlers by rubbing them on the tree trunk.

Chapter 3

Whooo Lives in That Tree?

Many other animals of the forest community live in the branches of the maple tree where the buck is cleaning its antlers. A spider has built a web high up in the leaves to catch flying insects. A moth, that is the same color as wood, stays still against the bark so that its enemies won't find it. A screech owl perches on a limb.

Screech owls are common animals in the temperate forest. The male and female look alike, except that the female is larger. The reddish or gray feathers have a pattern of dark and light colors. This helps make the owls almost invisible against the bark or branches of trees. They have large eyes that let them see far away. They have sensitive ears that pick up even the tiny sound of a mouse in the grass.

Screech owls fly very quietly.

Like all kinds of birds, a screech owl has feathers on its body and wings. The legs of the screech owl are covered with feathers, too. The screech owl even has feathers called tufts that stick up from the top of its head. Tufts have nothing to do with hearing, but scientists believe they are one way different kinds of owls can identify each other.

A screech owl's wing feathers are strong and firm. They are shorter and more rounded than most other birds' feathers. The edges of the feathers are soft, too. This is important, because it keeps the flight of an owl very quiet. While many birds' wings make swishing noises while flying, an owl's wing movements are almost completely silent. This helps the owl catch its **prey** by surprise.

Owls hunt many kinds of small animals in the forest. They are meat-eaters and dine on moths, grasshoppers, caterpillars, beetles, spiders, mice, salamanders, lizards, and even small birds and snakes. When it is through eating, the owl coughs up the parts of the meal it cannot digest in a small, tightly-packed pellet. These pellets litter the ground around the owl's nest.

Owl pellets contain the fur, feathers, and bones of its prey. Scientists have studied what owls eat by breaking apart the pellets and examining the clean, tiny skeletons of mice, rats, and other animals inside.

Owl pellets tell what an owl eats.

An owl's eyes do not move.

Screech owls, like most other owls, do not build fancy nests, but make their homes in places such as holes in tree trunks and branches. First, the male owl will hoot to learn if a territory is being used by another owl. If not, it will move in and claim the place as its own. Then the male will be joined by a female owl.

Screech owls seek out holes to build their nests in so that they are well hidden. Then their nest protects them from bad weather. Some screech owls whose territory is near the edge of the forest might nest in a building. They may even move into a birdhouse if the opening is big enough.

It is in the hollow of a maple tree that one female screech owl lays her eggs. She will lay one egg every two or three days until she has laid four or more. The eggs will take about 26 days to hatch. When the baby owls hatch, they are covered with soft white feathers called down. Soon, darker feathers grow in place of the down.

The babies stay in the nest for about a month. Each day the parents find food for them. The parents feed and protect the babies until they are old enough to leave.

One day when the owl family has left, the maple tree begins to shiver and shake. A tree cricket jumps to another tree. A stinkbug hangs on tightly to a leaf. Then the tree bends. The sound of bark cracking echoes in the forest. With a crash, the maple tree falls to the ground!

Chapter 4

Busy Builders

The maple tree has been cut down by nature's own best lumberjacks—beavers. They begin to chew apart the pieces of wood that will help make their own home.

Beavers of the North American temperate forests grow to be about as big as a large dog. A beaver's fur is brown. It has a broad head with powerful jaws. The beaver has 20 teeth. The four front teeth, called **incisors**, are used for cutting wood.

Beavers live in rivers or streams near forests. They spend some of their time on land but most of their time in water. Beavers are good swimmers and divers. They are busy animals. Beavers always seem to be working.

Beavers cut down trees to build their homes.

Beavers have short legs and black feet. Their front feet have long, thick claws, which they use to dig for food or to push water plants out of the way while swimming. Their back feet are larger than their front feet, and their toes are webbed. When beavers are in the water, their small noses close tight. A beaver can hold its breath for 15 minutes.

A beaver's tail is flat and looks like a paddle. A beaver uses its tail to steer while it is swimming. It uses its tail for balance so it can stand on its hind legs. It also uses its tail to **communicate** a warning to other beavers. It does this by slapping its tail on the water to make a loud noise.

Beavers build their lodges in streams or rivers.

Claws and sharp incisors allow beavers to do what they do best—cut down and section oak, maple, hickory, elm, and other trees. Beavers use the wood for several purposes. One is to build dams. The dams help stop up water in a stream or river so that it will become deeper and of more use. Another is to build **lodges** where beavers live.

A lodge looks a little like a teepee that is made of logs, branches, and mud. The top sticks out of the water. The lodge has several underwater openings and tunnels which lead to the inside chamber. The inside chamber is where beavers can dry off and stay warm when it is cold.

Even though beavers live on ponds and rivers, they do not eat fish. Instead, bark, twigs, leaves, and roots of trees and shrubs make up the beaver's diet. Beavers also like water plants, such as the roots and sprouts of water lilies.

Beavers do not hibernate in the winter, so they must store food for winter use. They do this by taking branches and logs underwater and anchoring them near their homes. In the winter, they swim under the ice and eat the bark from the branches and logs so they can survive until spring.

Beavers are excellent swimmers.

Baby beavers are born in April or May. They are called **kits**, or pups. A kit has soft, fluffy fur and can swim by the time it is only four days old. In two months its teeth are strong enough to eat the same food as full-grown beavers. A kit will live with its parents in the lodge until it is about two years old. Then it leaves to start a new life, either in the same stream or in a new place.

Many forest animals use the flooded areas created by beaver dams. Raccoons and skunks drink the water. Salamanders lay their eggs in the water. Frogs swim in the water. Sometimes, chipmunks stop by the water for a drink.

Chapter 5

Burrows and Pouches

One little chipmunk finishes its drink of water. Then it senses an owl nearby and quickly scampers back to hide in its **burrow**, where it lives. This small furry animal has a very good sense of smell, which helps protect it from **predators** who might want it for a meal.

A grown chipmunk is about eight inches (20 centimeters) long, including its tail. It has light-colored stripes bordered with black on its face, sides, and back. The rest of its fur is red-brown. These colors help the chipmunk hide in the leaves on the forest floor.

A chipmunk has sharp teeth and uses its front paws to hold nuts and seeds while it eats. It carries food in pouches inside its cheeks.

Chipmunks have sharp front teeth.

There are a variety of foods in the temperate forest for chipmunks. They search for nuts, such as acorns, beechnuts, and hickory nuts. Sometimes they bury the nuts the way squirrels do. Chipmunks also enjoy berries, seeds, and leaves. Once in a while a chipmunk might break off a mushroom and eat the top, but usually it just takes a few bites from a mushroom and leaves the rest alone. Insects such as butterflies, beetles, and grasshoppers are part of a chipmunk's diet. It also eats earthworms.

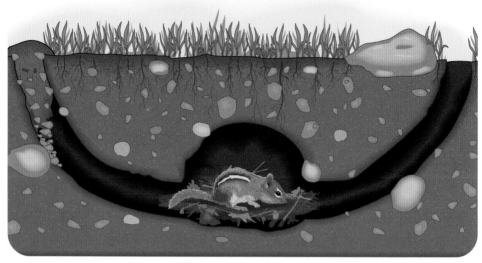

Chipmunks have underground burrows.

Chipmunks hibernate most of winter. They store nuts and seeds for when they wake. They hibernate underground in their homes. A chipmunk's home is a series of tunnels and rooms called a burrow. The chipmunk uses its paws for digging and kicking dirt. In this way, it **excavates** its home.

The entrance to a burrow is usually hidden, often beneath some brush, a pile of rocks, a woodpile, or a large tree root. The hole leading to the burrow is the size of the chipmunk itself—no larger. This keeps bigger predators out. The tunnels lead to rooms in which chipmunks store food and raise their babies.

Chipmunk babies are born in the spring. They are hairless and their eyes are closed. They stay in the burrow for about five weeks. First, they drink only milk. Later, their mothers give them seeds. By this time, their eyes have opened, they have grown hair, and they are active enough to go outside.

Young chipmunks stay close to the burrow, pouncing on each other and running back inside at the first sign of danger from predators such as screech owls. They may catch spiders and beetles for a snack. At six weeks, they are old enough to make their own homes and seek a hidden place to dig a burrow.

One young chipmunk spies a good place for a burrow—under a log a beaver has left behind. He begins to dig, eating some of the insects that crawl out of the log.

Chapter 6

T-T-Termites!

As the young chipmunk digs a new burrow beneath a log, there is something going on inside the log. A **colony** of termites is having a meal.

Termites are insects. Those in the temperate forest are small and live underground. There are three kinds of termites in a colony—royals, workers, and soldiers.

There are usually only two royal termites in a colony—a king and queen. It is their job to produce and lay eggs from which baby termites will hatch. They can make thousands of eggs a day!

Worker termites are small and have no wings and no eyes. Their bodies are white. Workers tend the nest by caring for the eggs and feeding the queen and the soldiers.

Workers also search for food and water with their sense of smell. They make tunnels in the nest as the colony grows larger.

Soldier termites are bigger than workers. Like workers, soldiers have no wings and are blind. They have very strong legs. It is the job of the soldiers to protect the colony against attacks from enemies, such as ants. To warn others in their colony of danger, soldiers will sometimes knock their heads against wood, making loud sounds. Soldier termites are unable to care for themselves and must be fed by the workers.

Termites make tunnels inside logs.

Worker termites care for the queen's eggs.

Termites have tunnels from their underground nests to their above-ground food source, such as the log. The tunnels let the termites move back and forth without having to go outside. Since termites live in moist, protected places, they do not have a hard covering on their bodies as many other insects do. If termites are left out in the air for very long, they will dry out and shrivel up.

Although termites eat wood, they cannot digest it. Inside each termite's body live **microscopic** creatures that help it digest the wood.

As the queen termite lays her eggs, workers carry them to cells in the nest and care for them. Newly-hatched termites are called **larvae**. Some larvae will develop into workers. Others will develop into soldiers or royals.

As the termites tunnel through the log, the wood becomes weaker and bits of it break off and fall to the ground. With time, these little bits of wood rot. They mix with other pieces of grass, moss, sticks, and tiny bits of rock. This mixture makes new soil. The new soil is important to the members of the forest community because this is where young flowers, shrubs, and trees will grow.

In the new soil near forest trees, a patch of red clover grows. A herd of deer comes and grazes on the leaves and buds. An owl hoots and flies into the tree's branches. If the tree falls down, a beaver quickly uses some of the wood to build a lodge in a stream. Then a chipmunk sips water from the stream and scurries into its home underneath the fallen tree. Termites inside the dead tree trunk have a meal of wood, which helps the tree to rot. The rotten bits of wood mix with rocks and sticks to make new soil. Then a new patch of clover begins to grow. Nature's circle is complete!

Chapter 7

The Forest Community and People

Everything in the temperate forest is important—every bird, every tree, every mushroom, and every termite. Each member of this community has a job to do that not only helps it survive but helps other living things survive, too. If any group of living things in the forest community is taken away, the whole community is affected.

The boy who lives by the forest goes to the store with his father. A carpenter comes to their house to repair a broken step. Across town, a doctor delivers a baby. In this community, too, the members have important jobs that help others. A community is a great place to live!

Glossary

burrow a hole or tunnel dug in the ground by an animal

colony a group of insects of the same kind living together

communicate to send a message with a signal

community all the living things in an area which often compete for or share what they need

excavate to dig out

herd a group of large animals which feed and live together

hibernate to pass the winter in a resting state

incisors front teeth

kit a baby beaver

larvae stage of development between egg and adult

lodge a beaver's den

microscopic so small a microscope is needed to see it

predator an animal which hunts other animals for food

prey an animal which is hunted by others for food

temperate mild

territory the area of land in which an animal lives

Index

beavers 17–21

burrow 22, 24–25

chipmunks 11, 22–25

community 3, 6, 29, 30

fawns 8

humans 3, 30

kits, beaver 21

lodge, beaver 19, 21

pellets, owl 14

royals, termite 26, 28

screech owls 12–16

soldiers, termite 26–28

temperate forest 3–6, 17, 23, 26, 30

termites 26–29

white-tailed deer 7–11

workers, termite 26–28